MW00772604

THE HIDDEN
LANGUAGE OF BUSINESS
WORKPLACE POLITICS, POWER & INFLUENCE
MARGARET MORFORD

COLD RIVER STUDIO
NASHVILLE, TENNESSEE

First Edition: June 2010

Printed in the United States of America
ISBN 978-0-9828146-0-4

ACKNOWLEDGEMENTS

I owe thanks to so many people who taught and shared with me the lessons offered in this book. Some of the lessons were amazingly insightful, some extremely painful, but all of them were life-changing. I have used real names whenever possible to give credit where credit is due.

Thank you, Dave, for agreeing a second time to the arduous task of editing my work, which involves nagging me weekly about getting chapters written. Grasshopper, once again you have given sparkle and magic to my words, without losing my voice in the process.

But the greatest thanks of all goes to my husband, Robert, one of the best managers I have ever encountered. You encourage me at every turn in my career (even when I think I cannot do something), teach me to see things from the other person's viewpoint (no matter how much I like my own), and make me laugh even in the darkest of times. I am grateful most managers are not like you or I would be out of a job! You are truly a remarkable man…and human being!

TABLE OF CONTENTS

INTRODUCTION

Being political has become synonymous with manipulating others or not telling the truth. Being "politically correct" suggests that we are doing or saying something a certain way because we have to. "Politics" has taken on a connotation of falseness and working in a political environment is seen as an experience to be avoided at all costs. But all these impressions are both naive and detrimental to anyone's working career. Unless you are a hermit living on a mountaintop in some remote area of the world, you deal with politics every day, and most especially at work. People who say they "don't play politics" are destined to fail. You cannot get two people together without politics taking place. Everybody has an agenda and everyone is trying to accomplish his or her agenda in the most efficient way possible.

Not a day goes by that we do not read in the news about an executive who has decided to resign "to pursue other interests" or "to spend more time with his family." Translation: he got fired. As people move up in the management ranks, they are rarely fired because of a lack of knowledge or ability. They usually are let go because they have made an enemy of someone powerful; or they have failed to pay attention to a subtle but critical change in the direction of their organization; or—more benign, but no less deadly—they have failed to build a wide enough network of supporters to carry them through when they make a mistake. Their organization usually offers some sort of reasonable explanation for their dismissal, but the real reason almost always lies in one of the above glaring political blind spots.

Since politics are inevitable in the workplace, wouldn't it be smart to become adept at not only dealing with them, but also understanding how to use them to accomplish your own work agenda? This book is *not* about stepping on people to get what you want out of your career. It *will* help protect you from those who would step on you to get what *they* want. This book is about practicing "positive politics" and succeeding…with your ethics and your soul intact.

I have come to see workplace politics as "the hidden language of business." Knowing this secret language allows you to operate with peak effectiveness in the workplace. And not knowing it—*not* possessing this crucial intelligence—easily can doom your career. By reading this book, you will gain exciting access to this hidden language—this inside intelligence—that is so critical to successfully navigating your career.

Ask yourself this: How many times at work have you been "right"—yet still made people mad? I know one person who was so "right" that her co-workers did not speak to her for a month! So it is "the hidden language of business"—the *positive office politics*—that will make or break your job satisfaction and advancement. Politics is the distinction between being merely right—and being *right and effective*. In any organization, being effective—in a positive, ethical way—is what really counts!

Politics isn't about winning at all costs. It's about maintaining relationships and getting results at the same time.
—John Elred

Chapter One

POLITICAL RULES
ABOUT YOU

The next six chapters will deal with political rules you either should not violate or that you should be actively following to enhance your career. When I began speaking on this topic several years back, there were only 25 political rules. I began with all the political mistakes I had made in my career—a few of which taught me lessons at a very high price. I then added all the political mistakes I had seen others make in the workplace. This book now covers 44 political rules. A few of the political rules may be obvious to you (They may have what I affectionately call "The Duh Factor."), but what is obvious to one person is often a light bulb moment for another. If you learn five new behaviors from this book, you will have moved your career along exponentially and significantly enhanced your effectiveness at work. As a consultant, I am in and out of 10 to 12 organizations per month. I see a lot of people striving to get their work done under a lot of different circumstances. I also see people getting politically "sideways" in their organizations—sometimes with career-ending results. The list of rules grows by one or two each year, as I have watched other individuals (with horror!) make other political mistakes. You cannot be politically tone-deaf and successful.

Throughout this book, as in my first one, I tell stories about my career, as well as other people's careers. I write about my own failures and successes, as well as those other people have shared with me. If a particular story illustrates a success, I use the person's real name, so he or she receives credit for the insight. On the other hand, if my story illustrates a difficult lesson or mistake, I have changed the name of the person in the story, to protect his or her privacy and dignity. I use life stories because they are the best illustrations of the organizational principles we are discussing. Not only are they interesting, but they take us from theory to real-world, from knowledge to actual application.

～•∾

Political Assignments to Enhance Your Career

As you go through each chapter of rules, circle the *one* from each chapter you are *most* likely to violate. You will have a tendency to want to circle more than one, but select the one you violate the *most*. At the end of Chapter Seven, you will have six rules circled. I will tell you what to do with them at the end of Chapter Seven. Keep reading and working, so you will begin to really master the art of positive politics.

——◦◦◦——

RULE #1:
Learn to say "yes" if at all possible.

The further up in an organization we move, the more we have a tendency to say "no." The more experience we get, the more we are able to avoid bad decisions or unsuccessful courses of action…and the more we want to help others avoid the painful mistakes we have made or have seen others make. With enough experience, we can see a train wreck coming about two sentences into someone's new idea or suggestion. Because of this, we often cut them short when we recognize what a waste of time it will be to pursue their suggestion. However, what we see as saving our employees, peers, and co-workers untold heartache, they often view as being inflexible and not open to new ideas—not a career-enhancing reputation in any organization.

Never kill anyone's bad idea or suggestion outright. Rather, let them abandon it as unworkable. The next time anyone at work wants to discuss a (bad) idea or suggestion, listen to the idea without interruption. Don't ask a question until they are completely finished explaining the idea because numerous questions do not suggest interest, but skepticism. Then say this: "We could do that. If we did, what should we do about _____?" Fill in the blank with the biggest flaw or your biggest objection to the idea and then shut up. The "Strategic Shut-Up" is one of the most powerful tools in your political tool kit. Staying silent is very difficult for most people in this situation because we are taught that polite people cover awkward silences in conversations—they do not create them. Nevertheless, you need to remain silent, allowing your employee, co-worker, or peer to work through the fact that their suggestion or idea isn't a very good one.

One of two things will happen at this point. First, the person you are speaking with may modify the idea or suggestion to overcome your objection, which may make it better and maybe workable. If they begin modifying the idea, the most I ever raise are three objections. If they can overcome my top three objections, I often go ahead and look at implementing the idea or suggestion. This process helps the employee, peer, or co-worker to think more practically or strategically, which means future ideas will be better.

The second possibility—and the most likely outcome—is that the employee, peer, or co-worker will be stumped by your question and unable to come up with a way to make the idea or suggestion work. At that point, you should let them off the hook by saying, "Why don't you think about that issue and come back to me when you have worked it out and we can discuss your idea further?" It is unlikely they will come back to see you again. In this way, they have killed their own suggestion or idea. You have not. You come across as someone who encourages suggestions and ideas.

Addendum to the rule—Do not ask the employee, peer, or co-worker, every time you see them, "How are you coming on that suggestion/idea?" If you do, you will be communicating time and again that it was a stupid suggestion or idea.

—∕∿∕—

RULE #2:
Do not talk about being "stressed out" or "burned out" at work.

People today seem to believe if they are not stressed out, they are not living and not working very hard. In fact, stress is fast becoming a status symbol. Because of this, people feel free to discuss workplace stress…in the workplace! While stress is very real and workplaces are extremely stressful these days—especially with the 24/7ness of voicemail, e-mail, text messaging, and tweeting—workplace stress should be discussed with your spouse, friends, counselor, or employee assistance program…not with the people who determine whether you get new assignments or promotions. Organizations do not promote people they believe cannot handle additional responsibilities, nor do they give exciting, new, and interesting assignments to people who are self-proclaimed "burn-outs."

—∕∿∕—

RULE #3:
Never cry or lose your temper at work.

I wish I didn't have to include this rule, but I see too much of this in the workplace. Lately, there has even been a rash of articles that say it is okay to cry at work. BUNK! It is okay to show your emotions at work (within reason), but it is never politically smart to cry in the workplace. When someone begins to cry, those around the "crier" scramble to do whatever they must to stop the crying. Often this means people either do what the crier wants or they quit doing what is making the person cry, even if it is providing valuable developmental feedback that could help the crier. Consciously or unconsciously, the crier gets what the crier wants from the situation. However, everyone who witnesses this behavior, or who hears that this person cried, forms the unconscious opinion that this person is weak or overly emotional. Organizations do not promote people they perceive to be weak. I have never cried at work. I have checked myself out for lunch at 10 o'clock in the morning, driven off the premises, and cried until I thought I would dehydrate myself, but I made sure when I returned no one could tell I'd had a good cry. If you don't take anything else from this book, please take this as your mantra: *I'm going to die before I cry!*

Currently, there is an executive coaching group that teaches it is okay for a member of senior management to lose his or her temper at work—but no more than twice a year. The explanation offered is that if they only do it twice a year, it will add great emphasis to their point of view. I am guessing this is a subtle way of getting senior managers to hold their tempers in check because the results can be devastating to an organization and to the senior executive. *Never* lose your temper at work—not once and certainly not twice.

Many times when you lose your temper at work, people will do what you want them to do, especially if you yell at them. However, as with crying, you win the battle, but lose the war. People develop the opinion that you are out of control or overly emotional—someone who is having trouble handling their current responsibilities. This makes them conclude that you should not be given any more responsibilities or be promoted because you might experience even more pressure and become more abusive.

I often get brought in to work with troubled senior executives. The trouble is usually a result of their particular management style. They cannot keep people working for them long-term and the organization cannot build an effective management team. The Board of Directors of one corporation had me work with their CEO because of an incident that occurred in his staff meeting. This meeting consisted of his direct reports and their direct reports—the 20 most powerful people in this organization. The CEO had assigned one of his female vice presidents the task of researching the possible change of a vendor for a service they outsourced. He simply wanted to see if they could get a better deal. The female VP liked the current vendor and had been dragging her feet about doing the project. He turned to her in all innocence in the meeting and asked, "Where are we on that project?" She had what I call a "come apart" right in the middle of the meeting, raised her voice, and told him, "I'm not doing it. It's stupid and a waste of my time. There is nothing wrong with our current vendor and we don't need to change. I'm busy and I have better things to do." Not only did she say this, but she got right up in his face and started poking him in the chest. He lost his temper and called her a couple of names, including the C-word.

When he appeared in the conference room, looking as if

he would rather be hanged than spend the day working with me, he asked, "Didn't they tell you what she did?" I assured him they did. "Then why are we spending all this money and time dealing with me?"

"Well," I replied, "the problem is that you had a lot of options in this situation and you chose the one course of action that leaves you *no* options. Your female VP was insubordinate when she told you she was not doing the project—in front of 18 witnesses, no less! Insubordination is a fireable offense in any organization. She also committed assault and battery when she poked you in the chest. Again, a fireable offense. She gave you two perfectly justifiable reasons to fire her if you determined she was not on your team. I am going to show you another option you had, where you could have retained her because of her knowledge, but made her back down so publicly that she would never challenge you again, nor would anyone else in the room. You squandered all your options because you lost your temper. Because you did, your female VP is pretty much untouchable now. She has a job in your organization for as long as she wants it and can continue to challenge your authority and not worry about the consequences. And worse for you, everyone knows it."

In this case, losing his temper had put the CEO on the hot seat regarding his career and given the insubordinate VP an upper hand and a golden parachute.

—⟨∅∅∅⟩—

RULE #4:
Never reveal your insecurities or shortcomings to your boss or co-workers.

It is amazing how many times I hear a manager say something nice about someone's work and the employee does not know how to handle the compliment. Instead of simply saying "thank you," they counter the compliment by pointing out one of their flaws such as saying, "Well, you know I'm not very organized." If your manager hasn't noticed the flaw, for Pete's sake, do not point it out!

When your manager says something nice about you, you are not required to balance the scales by saying something negative about yourself. Take your kudos and run! Heaven knows they come rarely enough in the workplace! In addition, you can triple the chances that your boss will say something nice about you again by saying, "Thank you so much! That means a great deal to me coming from you." (Emphasize the word *you* just slightly.) Then practice your Strategic Shut-Up!

—⟨∅∅∅⟩—

RULE #5:
Do not discuss your salary or special job perks with anyone at work.

When your manager does something nice for you as a reward for your hard work, you may want to tell everyone.

It may be in the form of some special training, getting you appointed to a special project team, sending you to a seminar, etc. Resist the temptation to tell any of your co-workers. Besides the risk of having your co-workers dislike you, think about what your boss experiences when you tell others. Invariably, your manager will be quizzed by your co-workers about why you are getting the special treatment. Someone may even be bold enough to accuse your boss of favoritism. Clearly, your supervisor is going to defend the decision by pointing out that you always stay late or take on additional responsibilities without being asked. (At least I hope your boss will not miss this opportunity to show your co-workers what types of behaviors earn additional perks!) After offering that explanation a few times, valid though it may be, managers begin to wish they had never done this wonderful thing for their employee because they have bought themselves so much hassle by doing so. That is not a frame of mind that will earn you additional perks in the future. So take your perks, practice your Strategic Shut-Up, and run!

—◦◦◦—

RULE #6:
Avoid discussing your personal and/or health problems, unless absolutely necessary, and then only on a need-to-know basis.

I am over 50 as I write this, so I feel fortunate that body parts are not dropping off me every day! As people age, they become increasingly more preoccupied with all aspects of their health. If you ever get together with a group of people, you often feel as if you are sitting through a symptom competition—complete with excruciating details. The truth of the matter is that your health is only fascinating to you. People at work are listening simply to be polite (or they are waiting for their turn to report). Even your doctor does not find your health interesting. You have to pay him or her to listen to your symptoms! Believe me, after you have spent 15 minutes describing your hemorrhoid surgery to me, I am never going to look at you the same way again!

With the advent of all the talk shows, reality TV, and self-help programs, people feel they can discuss their personal problems freely and with no editing. We may watch those shows with morbid fascination, but those discussions have no place in the workplace. While tales of your crazy family members and your personal crisis may garner you some short-term sympathy, they also will make people, at best, question your discretion, trustworthiness, and confidentiality. At worst, they may make people question your sanity, as the apple never falls far from the crazy family tree. Work is not therapy. Do not treat it as such.

—◦◦◦—

RULE #7:
Keep confidences, unless they are violations of your organization's ethics.

We have all experienced the person at work who comes and wants to tell us something, but wants to swear us to secrecy, wants it to be "off the record," or wants to tell us as their "friend" and not a member of management. If you are a manager, you have neglected your legal obligations to your organization if someone tells you certain things in confidence and you do not report them. You also may accrue some personal liability for this failure to act. (And if you are not a manager, you do not want to be walking around knowing someone, especially a friend, is being unfairly treated without being able to help him or her report it.) You have lots of competing interests in these situations. If this person is being discriminated against or harassed, you want to know about it so your organization can address it. You do not want to do anything that will discourage reporting these situations. Also, you want to preserve your honor and reputation for being able to keep anyone's confidences or secrets, if they choose to share them with you. The best way to straddle that line and meet all these competing interests is to say to the person, "You know, I'll keep your confidences as much as humanly possible, but there are some few (emphasize the word *few* just slightly) things that I have to do something about, if I become aware of them. For instance, if you tell me someone is stealing, I have to report that. Understanding there are some few things like that, tell me what is bothering you and I will do whatever I can to protect your confidences and to help you." In my 20 years of management experience, I have never had anyone that did not go on and tell me what was on their mind. If it turned out to be a concern about harassment or discrimination, I would tell the individual, "This is one of those things *we* have to report. How do you want to do that?"

Do not give the individual a long laundry list of the things you have to report. Use the theft example. It is clear and leaves the door cracked for you to report, if you need to. At the same time, it helps you keep your word to the person who has come to talk with you.

━━⊷∽∾⊶━━

RULE #8:
Do not become romantically involved with anyone in your chain-of-command.

This seems so obvious, but often when the heart desires, the brain takes a vacation. Have I read the studies that say at least 80 percent of the people in the workforce have dated someone with whom they work? Absolutely! Next to eHarmony and Match.com, the workplace is the best place to meet someone once you get out of school. I am not saying you cannot date someone with whom you work, but I do not recommend it. I especially do not recommend it if that person is in your chain-of-command. Never mind the legal troubles you create for your organization regarding potential sexual harassment suits. You also put a question in everyone's mind about your abilities. No matter how competent or smart you are, if you have a relationship with someone who has a modicum of power, people will never believe that you advanced on your own merit. Many will say you got where you got because of your personal relationship. You give anyone who is jealous of your success the opportunity to denigrate or nullify your achievements simply because of your personal behavior. This is especially true if you are a woman. As one of my old warhorse managers used to say: "Don't fish off the company dock!"

—⌘—

RULE #9:
Drink in moderation at all functions or gatherings where other employees are present.

Think of all the people who choose the company holiday party to cut loose because some, if not all, the alcohol was paid for by their employer. Their behavior is all everyone talks about at work during the week after the party. You cannot erase the picture of you dirty dancing to the latest Justin Timberlake song from people's memories. While it is not fair and has nothing to do with your work performance (except for sexual harassment liability you may have created for your employer—an assured career-advancement killer!), there now exists for all time (or at least for several years following the incident) a question about your lack of control and judgment …something that will keep you from being promoted or given additional responsibility.

I once worked with a brilliant vice president of marketing. When she arrived at the annual holiday party, her husband clearly had been drinking. As the evening progressed, he had several more drinks and proceeded to pressure many of the young women who worked for the VP to dance with him. He rubbed suggestively against three or four of them on the dance floor. He even attempted to reach down the dress of one particularly attractive direct report of hers. Monday morning began with a parade of the young women going to Human Resources, complaining that they were subjected to this behavior, that they were not comfortable refusing to dance with him because he was the spouse of their boss, and wanting to know what the company was going to do to address the behavior. In this case, the company had to call in the VP and tell her that if anything like this happened again, they would have to ban her husband from all company functions. Of more concern to the VP should have been the many questions about her judgment in showing up at a company function with her husband having had too much to drink, in not monitoring her husband's drinking once she got there, and, ultimately, in not monitoring her husband's behavior at the party.

In addition to company functions, this rule applies to cutting loose during non-work time with co-workers. Regardless of how stressful your workweek has been, it is a bad idea to have one drink too many while out with co-workers after hours, or even on a Friday or Saturday night. While you are on your own time, you can bet that at work on Monday morning everyone will be talking about the indiscreet opinion of someone in senior management you expressed or, at worst, that you were dancing on the bar. And ladies, if you have any piece of lingerie nailed up at a bar anywhere in your town, it is time to relocate and start your career fresh in another town.

Chapter Two
POLITICAL RULES ABOUT YOUR CAREER

—⟡⟡⟡—

RULE #10:
Network once every week with someone outside your organization.

You need to build a wide network of supporters outside your organization as well as internally. You should start doing this today, rather than at a point in your career when you need help or assistance. This will not happen by accident. You are going to have to *purposefully* invest 15 minutes each week in building your external network. Once per week, you should open your address book, business card file, electronic rolodex, phone (or wherever you keep business contact information), close your door and spend 15 minutes on the telephone talking with one person outside your organization. Do not ask for anything. Simply tell them you were thinking about them and wondered how they are doing. Not only will this be a nice break in your day, but it will strengthen your relationship with a business contact who may eventually have the next piece of business you want, be the next person you want to recruit for your organization, be the next vendor you want excellent terms from, or have the next job you want.

We have all received telephone messages from people we have not heard from in years, saying they just want to catch up. You know when you call them back, they are going to want something. I usually find they are looking for a new job and want to do some networking. I am happy to help anyone looking for work. I will make suggestions for places to contact and people to call. However, when the person who calls me twice a year just to see how I am doing asks for help, I do not *just* make suggestions. I work my network, making phone calls and introductions to open as many doors as possible for them.

With the advent of downsizing, reorganizations, and acquisitions, employment is uncertain. If 80% of the jobs in this country are gotten by someone who knows somebody who knows someone else, you need a wide network to help you identify great opportunities that never hit the job boards or newspapers—the ones you hear about only when an organization announces that so-and-so is coming aboard to fill a great job you never even knew was open!

———&———

RULE #11:
Keep your resume updated at all times.

There is an interesting phenomenon that occurs with managers who have to fill a position. They want to fill the open position as soon as possible, with as little work as possible, so they can return to the work that needs to be done in their department. They do not want to launch a huge job search, because it takes away from what they see as their *real* job. If they find a resume with qualifications they really like, they mentally hire that person for the position before they even start the interview process. In talent management, I call this the "Curse of the Pre-Selected Candidate." As long as their pre-selected candidate does not do anything too outrageous in the face-to-face interview, the manager will hire him. Managers are so averse to an exhaustive interview process that (I am convinced) I could tell a manager the pre-selected candidate ax-murdered his last manager and my manager would chalk it off to a communication problem—and still want to hire him!

If you are smart, you can take advantage of this reluctance to do any intensive interviewing and try to make yourself the pre-selected candidate. However, you cannot do that if your resume is not ready at a moment's notice. When you hear about a new opportunity, send your resume immediately, to get your credentials in front of the hiring manager before she looks at many other resumes. Once the hiring manager finds her pre-selected candidate, your resume will not have as much impact, so it is important to get your resume in front of the manager early in the process. The fact that you sent your resume so quickly leaves the hiring manager with the impression that you are extremely responsive, as well as very interested in the position. You also will benefit from the fact that—once a manager has a pre-selected candidate in mind—she quits aggressively telling other people about the position, because she has already mentally filled it. So you will limit the number of people against whom you have to compete for the position!

—◦◦◦—

RULE #12:
Write an annual accomplishments list and publish it to those higher up in your organization. Quantify those accomplishments with numbers or percentages.

What are you worth to your employer? If you do not know the answer, your employer doesn't either! Sure, your employer knows you are valuable, but in this era of strained budgets and cost-cutting initiatives, you need to be able to quantify what you are worth every year. In one company where I worked, our department did this each year, simply because we were an administrative department and got tired of everyone thinking we were a drain on the bottom line.

The process is simple. Make a list of the major things you have accomplished for the year. Determine the cost your organization would have incurred if you had not accomplished each task. Give a one-line description of the accomplishment and then list to the right its value in dollars. If you cannot assign a dollar value to it, do not report it. Always estimate conservatively, so if someone challenges your numbers they will hold up. Otherwise, this will backfire and you will look like someone who pads his or her resume.

Do not tell yourself you cannot translate your business actions into hard dollars. If you tell yourself that, you most certainly will be the first department to suffer cost cuts when times get tough. You want your organization to see any reduction in your role or department as a huge loss to the bottom line.

Here are a few examples of things that may seem unquantifiable at first, but which can be extremely valuable if you do a little research:

If you reduce turnover by two percentage points from last year to this year, figure out what it costs to hire and train someone new and calculate the savings. (Do not use the national average, but, rather, the real savings for your organization.) Pay particular attention to positions that require special expertise (e.g., engineers, computer programmers, scientists) or long training curves (e.g., any sales position, because you have to teach people your products, services, and pricing structure no matter how much sales experience they have as they join your organization). If your benefits costs will rise 12% for the coming year, but you revise the plans or bid your business out to a new provider and the increase is only nine percent, what is the cost difference to your organization?

Perhaps you reduced your legal claims from last year to this year. Figure out what the average cost of a claim is and multiply it by the number you reduced from the previous year. Look at the decrease in attorneys' fees you are paying to resolve problems you are now taking care of internally. Also, any state training funds or grants you obtain for your organization are bottom-line dollars and should be reported. List all your items with the number to the right, and then in capital letters, bolded at the bottom of the page, write "Grand Total for 20XX" and put the number to the right. This will certainly get people's attention.

The first year our department did this, we sent out one sheet (five accomplishments that year) to each member of senior management. Our CEO (a former CFO) came to my office and said, "I reviewed your numbers and I had no idea your department was worth $1.1 million last year."

That stuck in his mind the entire next year—which is exactly what you want stuck in any senior executive's mind about your department. After we saw the positive results that first year, we did it every year after that. It became easier each year because we recorded our accomplishments in a file as they happened. It simply became a matter of writing up the pertinent things from the file we had been keeping all year.

If you are going to do this individually, do it at the same time each year, but strategically time the release of the information. We did our list every January—right after the year was complete. It was an easy time to do it. Even more important, January was right before the budget process began, which included raise recommendations for everyone in the department. Get your list to your manager right before they begin writing your annual review. You can help your manager write a better review if you arm them with powerful financial facts. This also will help your manager obtain a good raise or promotion for you.

—————

RULE #13:
Have your business cards with you at all times.

People squander lots of great opportunities because they do not have business cards with them in non-business situations. You may meet your organization's next big customer at your child's Little League baseball game. You may be sitting next to the next great employee for your company traveling on an airplane. You may meet the next vendor with whom your company should do business serving on a charity board. Most importantly, you may meet the next person you want to work for or be mentored by at a neighborhood barbecue. No matter what the circumstances, it is always appropriate to say, "I have really enjoyed our conversation and would like to swap business cards with you." Having your business card available under any circumstances leaves the other person with the impression that you are professional and constantly prepared.

Common courtesy demands that the other person, in turn, gives you their business card, which allows you to follow-up on your conversation. Now you have some control over that interaction. If the person you have met does not have a business card with him, simply take another of your business cards out, flip it over, and say, "Why don't we turn my business card into yours? Will you give me your contact information?"

You never want a good contact to slip away from you, nor do you want to be dependent upon the other person to make the first move.

—◆◆◆—

RULE #14:
Save three to six months of salary as fall-back money.

This rule got added to my list because of a conversation I had with a young professional named Mike Thompson. When we were discussing a particularly turbulent time his company was experiencing, I asked if he thought he would be okay when all the dust settled. He told me he would be okay no matter how it turned out because he had his "Go to Hell Fund" (his words, not mine, but very descriptive!). He talked about the fact that, early on in his career, he made himself save a little each paycheck until he had saved six months' worth of salary. Once he had done that, he noticed that when everyone else was out of control, stressed, and doing silly things—jockeying for position when it was obvious a change was in the works—he remained calm, sane, professional, and efficient. He believes that, on at least two occasions, it made new owners decide to keep him, rather than lay him off. It also enables him to sleep at night, no matter what is going on at work, and makes him incredibly stress-resilient. In one case, I believe it got him promoted because he clearly could handle more, no matter what the pressure.

In addition, Mike told me, it gives him choices. Often, you get asked as a manager to support and/or execute initiatives you do not personally like or feel are inappropriate for your organization. He explained that when he was faced with these types of situations, "I would ask myself, 'Am I so opposed to this that I am willing to use my Go to Hell Fund to look for a new job?' The answer almost always is 'no,' but at least I get to make a choice. It drives my stress level down and ultimately reminds me that I always have choices."

—⦿⦿⦿—

RULE #15:
Learn one new job skill every year.

If you are not getting smarter or more talented every year, you are getting stale and less employable. There is a huge difference between having 10 years of experience and having the same year of experience 10 times! You have to plan for development. It will not just happen because you are busy doing the mammoth amount of work your job requires. Make a decision now! What new job skill are you going to learn in the next 12 months? For example, will you take a finance course, which is what I did one year, in order to become more adept at understanding the balance sheet in your organization?

This does not have to be a formal class. You can volunteer for a temporary assignment in another department of your organization or volunteer to serve on a committee that involves other areas of the organization. A good test for whether you are sharpening your skills adequately each year is to ask yourself:

"If I updated my resume annually, would I have something new to add to it?" If the answer is "no," you need to really concentrate on making this happen immediately. (See Rule # 11—"Keep Your Resume Updated at All Times.")

———

RULE #16:
Become active in one or two professional associations or boards.

There are two important aspects to this rule. First, choose *only* one—two at the most—boards to serve on. If you choose more than that, you will be ineffective on all of them. When I see on anyone's resume five board positions listed, I know they are making no impact, have no real desire to serve, and are really just into collecting data for their resume. None of which makes me want to hire them. I once had an applicant who put on her resume she was on the board of the local Red Cross. I looked up the board members and called the president of the board for a reference. The president had a hard time even placing who the individual was. "I think she's the one we see only a few times a year at meetings," he said. It is very telling to me how hard someone works when he or she is not being paid!

When you do need an employment reference, do not miss the opportunity to encourage prospective employers to call your fellow board members, telling them, "I am using my board service as a reference because I thought it might give you some idea of my work ethic. Regardless of what I am paid, once I sign on, I give it everything I can." There is no more compelling reference.

———⟨◦◦◦⟩———

RULE #17:
Be careful not to price yourself out of the market for your current position.

This rule came to me from a news director for a multiple-station television broadcast group. Each television station in his group has a news director and his particular group required employment contracts from all senior managers. His employment contract was up for renewal and he called to run a strategy for negotiation past me. He said he was thinking about *not* asking for a raise this contract period. He was one of the highest paid news directors in his group because he was particularly smart and innovative and had been rewarded in the past for his results. His biggest fear was that the group would be sold and he would stick out as a huge salary expense to any new owners, who would not know how superior his talents were. If the group did not sell, but needed to do some expense cutting, again he might attract unwanted attention. He told me that if he asked for the norm in his company, he could probably get about a $5,000 increase that year. However, he was thinking about asking not for an increase, but instead, for an additional week of vacation and to be sent to the Poynter Institute for a week. In journalism, attending the Poynter Institute is the equivalent of attending Harvard.

"What would the total cost to your company be to send you to the Poynter Institute?" I asked.

"About $10,000 in all, when you count in travel expenses, books, tuition, etc.," he replied.

I told him I thought it was a brilliant strategy because the week of vacation was easily worth $2,000 to him. He would now get about $12,000 worth of value, very little of which the IRS could tax, instead of a $5,000 annual increase that the IRS could fully tax. Then, if the worst happened and his job got eliminated somewhere down the road, he would have the Poynter Institute to put on his resume.

If your company is in the position of having few, if any, dollars available for raises, consider asking for something else instead of a raise. This will relieve some economic pressure on your organization, make you appear to be a team player, and allow you to channel your energies toward something more psychologically fulfilling than a small raise that the IRS will take a big bite out of.

Consider asking for any of the following:

- Additional time off beyond the current paid-time-off policy.
- Five workdays per year devoted to community service. You get paid and your organization gets credit for being a good corporate citizen.
- Being allowed to attend (and work) the big convention for your industry. This is a great way to rub shoulders with some of the highest-level executives in your organization, meet some of your biggest customers, and make great contacts

in your industry. These conventions are always held in nice cities at nice hotels, and organizations.
always need an extra pair of hands at the conference.

- Serving on a board in your company's name and during company time. Again, you will make great contacts and your employer will pay your dues.
- Working from home a certain number of days per week. What you save in gas probably will compensate for any raise you surrender.

Remember, politics is about negotiating smart, not necessarily more.

—◦◦◦—

RULE #18:
Post-mortem your performance at your old job right before you start a new job.

When you leave one organization for another, you should spend a little time soul-searching before you begin with the new organization. Changing jobs gives you an opportunity to start fresh. You should not waste the chance to examine your old mistakes—to look at anything you could have done better—so you can achieve better performance results in the future. This way, you are not destined to make the same types of missteps again. Abandon asking whether your decisions or methods were right, and ask what you could have done to be more effective.

Here is an example that illustrates this rule:

I know one very sharp woman who has become virtually

unemployable because she refuses to change her method of operation. She has been fired or pushed out of her last three jobs. She is smart and a good, hard worker. You can give her a department that is exceptionally messed up and she will have it running like a top and profitable within six months.

Her huge political mistake is that she always forges excellent relationships with her bosses, but never bothers with her peers or direct reports. Everything works great for her and she gets lots of raises and autonomy, until her boss moves on and she no longer has that support. Everyone then bad-mouths her to the new boss or regime, and she is usually out of a job within 30 days of her old boss' departure, despite the fact that she saved her last organization in excess of a million dollars over the last three years.

Each time this has happened to her, I have waited until she landed a new job before suggesting we post-mortem her last job. (You wait until the person has a new job to have this discussion because you do not want to discourage them during a job search, when they need to be positive, self-confident, and strong.) She always says she understands about building a wide network at each new job, but invariably she goes back to her old way of doing things, because it is fast, efficient, effective at getting results, and impresses her new boss quickly. Because she has been let go three times now, prospective employers are very leery of hiring her. Last time I spoke with her, she had been out of work for more than a year, with no prospects on the horizon.

I initially learned this political rule through my own bitter experience. In one of my earlier jobs, I handled the toughest employee relations situations for managers because I was adept at handling them and at keeping my company from being sued. I fired people for managers because I knew they would mess it up if they did it. Everything I did was in the best interest of my company, but I came to understand that all the bad things that happened to employees in our company had one thing in common—*me!* That was the reputation I had acquired because all managers would allow me to step in and do the hard work for them. In addition, they never learned to do the hard stuff well because I was always waiting in the wings to do it for them. When someone needed to talk to the CEO about something he was not going to like, I always volunteered so that I would be seen as courageous. (When the CEO exploded, my peers were nowhere to be found!)

As I began my next job, it was real growth for me when I said to one of my peers, "You know, if you feel that strongly about it, why don't *you* go talk to the CEO?" Your focus needs to be on not just doing the right thing, but in building the right reputation at the same time.

Ask yourself: What is my reputation in my current organization? What does each constituency group (your boss, your peers, your direct reports, etc.) believe about me? If you are "sideways" with any of these groups or feared rather than respected, you need to change the way you relate to each one. If you have been in your organization a significant length of time, you may need to consider changing jobs, even if you do not want to, because it is very hard to change a negative perception that has become fixed in people's minds. It is often easier to start over somewhere else and to craft a completely new image for yourself.

Chapter Three
POLITICAL RULES ABOUT YOUR PERSONAL COMMUNICATION

———⟡⟡⟡———

RULE #19:
Listen to the grapevine.

Dozens of studies about corporate culture reveal you *have* to be plugged into your organization's "grapevine." That's how you discover what is *really* going on, how high or low employee morale *really* is, and what is *really* going to happen in the future. One CEO I know calls this the "corporate underground." Eighty percent of what you hear on the grapevine has an element of truth to it. You need to know what is being said—even if it is not true—to respond to the rumor mill and put a stake in the heart of poisonous rumors so they cannot rise again.

You also must watch for an informal grapevine I call "the meeting after the meeting" (MAM). This is a meeting that takes place almost immediately after a large corporate announcement about a new initiative or program. A small group of influential "doers" will get together after the meeting to determine how much of the new initiative or program they are *really* going to enact. More organizational change has been stymied in this informal meeting than anywhere else in the process, and organizations are usually clueless as to why the change failed.

You want to be a part of the MAM. Begin to notice who breaks off into what groups after the official meeting. The MAM group usually has several people in it that will be critical to implementing any change. In the next official meeting, be sure to sit next to one of these individuals. As the meeting breaks up, fall into step with that individual and casually walk out with him or her, all the way to the MAM. Pick a different person each meeting and do the same thing. Do not say anything in the MAM—just listen. You want people to get used to seeing you at the MAM. After you have done this three times, you will be viewed as a regular member of the group and can begin speaking up.

—⟨⟨⟨⟩⟩⟩—

RULE #20:
Listen more than you speak.
Say as little as possible.

I learned this rule through one of the most painful experiences of my career. I had gone to work for an organization that was part of a multi-company conglomerate. I was lucky enough to work for the only CEO in all the companies who believed the head of Human Resources should report directly to him. Because of that, I was part of the senior management team and attended weekly staff meetings, unlike my counterparts in the other companies.

Six months into my tenure, I realized my peers did not see me as a legitimate member of senior management. As a matter of fact, they worked on other things when I spoke in the meetings—because they did not care what I had to say! But my worst, most painful realization was: *It was all my fault.*

Here's why:

Because nearly everything we discussed had a human resources component to it, I commented on nearly everything. I talked and I talked and I talked. I finally realized my associates heard nothing I said . . . because I said *so much.*

I decided to sit through the next senior management meeting without saying a word. I had to push veins back into my head once or twice, but I discovered that, 75 percent of the time, my peers would get where I needed them to get on an issue without my saying anything. It might take them three times as long and was painful to watch, but they made the decision I would have recommended. Most important, it was *their* decision. It was no longer me forcing them to do the right thing. The other 25 percent of the time, I would let them wear themselves out discussing what was clearly an issue in my area. When they finally wound down, I would wait two seconds and say, "I have a different take on that." Because I spoke so rarely in these meetings, they would give much more weight to my advice and were very likely to do what I recommended. Use your words sparingly, so they get treated with greater value when you *do* speak.

—◦◦◦—

RULE #21:
Always meet in someone else's office to control what happens in the meeting.

This is both a time management suggestion and a political one. Always go to see anyone in their office when you want to keep the conversation short. This is especially true regarding people in your organization who are "windy." Start the meeting by asking for the information you need. Then start rising out of your chair the minute you have that information, thanking them for their time. They are likely to wind up the conversation fairly quickly. (It is not nearly as easy to get them to leave when they are sitting in *your* office.)

From a political standpoint, it is more effective to negotiate with people in their offices. All the books on power tell you exactly the opposite—that you should make people come to your office because that is your power base and they will feel uncomfortable and make more concessions there. BUNK! The authors of those books are only thinking about one aspect of human psychology. Here's another: Long before you entered the work force, your parents taught you to be nice to your guests. In many cases, you were taught to do what guests wanted because they were "company." That training was drilled bone-deep into most of us. As the line between one's work and personal life has become almost nonexistent, people have come to unconsciously think of their offices as an extension of their homes, and all that stuff from childhood applies! So while you are sitting behind your desk telling yourself how powerful you are, I have usually gotten at least one concession out of you because I am your guest.

—⦾⦾⦾—

RULE #22:
Avoid closing your door unless it's absolutely necessary.

Whenever anyone with a modicum of power closes their door, people begin to whisper things like, "*Something's going on.*" And the "something" is never anticipated to be positive. In the absence of information, it is human nature to fill a void with negative speculations. These can run the gamut from "people are getting laid off" to "the company is being sold." In fact, the most *positive* negative speculation people may have is that you are not working. Or that you are looking for a new job. Even if you *are* looking for a new job, you do not want anyone to suspect it. It is simply not good for you or your organization. And remember: The higher up you are in your organization, the more negative any speculation will be—and the bigger the panic. So don't fuel panic—and possibly drive some of your best employees out the door—by letting people falsely conclude that your workplace is volatile or that something really awful is about to happen.

When I first started managing, whenever employees asked to see me, I shut my door to afford them privacy. I soon realized I was sending the wrong message to others: That I was unapproachable, unavailable, and too busy to help them. Now, when employees ask to see me, I greet them and invite them into my office. If they choose to shut the door, that is fine. Or if they start to discuss something private, I ask them to stop a minute, and then I get up to close my door, telling them, "I want to give you any privacy you need to discuss this matter with me."

Several things happen because of this: I bolster my reputation for having an open-door policy. I enhance my reputation for confidentiality. I engage in good time management because open-door discussions are briefer. Finally, I convey that I welcome input from everyone.

If you must close your door to limit interruptions because you are trying to get a project finished, find an empty office or conference room in which to work. Leave your office door open, to send the message that you are available and approachable and that things are going well in your organization.

———ↄⱷⱷↄ———

RULE #23:
Watch side conversations and do not check messages in meetings.

Often, when people sit in the back of a meeting or halfway down the conference table, they mistakenly believe they have disappeared. But the person running the meeting, standing at the front of the room or at the head of the conference table, has a vantage point three feet higher than other attendees. So they see people working on other things, whispering to each other, or writing notes to each other. They also are not fooled that some attendees are having a silent moment of prayer because their heads are bowed. They realize these people are checking their phone or PDA. This is a huge mistake. These individuals are sending the unspoken message to the person running the meeting—who usually is far more powerful in the organization than they are—that what the person is saying is not important or they do not care . . . both of which are deadly messages to convey!

Addendum to the rule—Never go to a meeting, training session, seminar or presentation without a pen and something to write on. You are sending an unspoken message (or multiple messages) that you are either not interested, don't believe the speaker has anything interesting to say, are disengaged, or are too lazy to take notes.

—◦◦◦—

RULE #24:
Understand the value of telling your story first.

There are 50 different ways to describe why and how a workplace conflict occurred, with each of them being accurate. So when you have a disagreement with someone, do not wait until the dust settles. Manage the conflict quickly and effectively. When anyone gets angry at you, or vehemently disagrees with you, think about to whom they will go to complain about the situation. Here is a hint: It will usually be their manager or your manager. If you share a boss, it is *obvious* where they will go! So go to their boss and tell him or her, "Susie just left my office and was very upset. She wants to do _____ and here is why I thought that course of action was unwise." When Susie meets with her boss, you have given that person the ammunition he or she needs to defend you. It is difficult for Susie to argue her position effectively when she hears *your* justifications coming out of *her* manager's mouth. If her boss disagrees with you and wholeheartedly supports Susie, you are still better off knowing that. Why? Because you can then go to Susie in private and work it out one-on-one, rather than be disagreed with publicly in a large meeting.

—◦◦◦—

RULE #25:
Deliver bad news face-to-face.

With the advent of today's technology (voicemail, e-mail, text messaging, etc.), it is possible to keep people at bay almost all the time and never have an actual, face-to-face conversation. This greatly reduces the hassle factor in the workplace, but also keeps people from being supporters of yours or from feeling like a part of your team and doing everything they can to make you successful. We are especially tempted to use these methods of communication when we suspect the person will be angry with the news we are delivering—and likely will spew that anger back at us (a.k.a., "shooting the messenger").

If you have negative news for co-workers, go see them and begin the conversation by saying, "You are not going to like what I am about to tell you, but I respect you too much not to come tell you in person." You have now achieved two things:

> *(1)* You have prepared them for bad news, so they are less likely to be surprised and therefore angry at you. Most people lose their tempers when they are surprised by something they did not expect to happen. This is why people use the expression "flash of anger." Because you have prepared the recipient for the negative message ahead of time, you have given them not only a warning about the nature of what is coming next, but a minute to steel themselves for the bad news.

(2) You have cultivated your co-worker's respect for you because they will realize that you had an easy way (voicemail or e-mail) to avoid a reaction, which you refused to take. You now can expect a much calmer response, along the lines of: "You're right. I'm not happy about the decision, but I appreciate your coming to talk directly with me about it." You are simply asking for respect equal to what you have shown the person. Most people like fairness and balance and will respond accordingly.

Your co-workers can make or break your career. Be politically savvy enough to go *beyond* being simply collegial. *Work* those relationships so they benefit you and those who work for you.

If it is impossible to meet face-to-face, call the person so they can hear the tone of your voice, the cadence, and the speed at which you speak. If a huge time-zone difference separates you and the other person, get up in the middle of the night to make the call so the recipient will know how important they are to you. Only seven percent of communication comes from the words we use. The rest is voice tone, body language, and facial expression. So meeting face-to-face—or calling, if you have to—allows you to communicate much more effectively and completely.

Chapter Four

POLITICAL RULES ABOUT YOUR ELECTRONIC COMMUNICATION

———⟨⟨⟩⟩———

RULE #26:
Avoid saying anything negative in an electronic document.

No matter what you say about someone, it carries greater weight when you say it in writing. And it lives forever—or at least long enough for the wrong person to see it! This is why employers put corrective action in writing. Not because they want to "get" someone, but because people pay attention when it is there in black and white. Electronic communication never really goes away. In fact, the Federal Rules of Evidence now require employers to keep all electronic communication for a period of time, even when employees have deleted it from their systems and emptied it from their electronic trash cans. There are forensic specialists who make a living recovering this stuff. Attorneys jokingly refer to electronic communications as "Exhibit A." So be aware of this—because, in any lawsuit against your employer, you do not want to be the person who created Exhibit A for the plaintiff or prosecution! (To further complicate things, a study by the American Bar Association reveals 76 percent of jurors believe managers will lie to protect their jobs. But they believe documentation almost 100 percent of the time—no matter who created it.)

People today treat electronic communication as if it were the same as conversation. It is not! It is nothing but a never-ending, almost eternal trail of thoughts and feelings that, in most cases, are better left unsaid. If you must say something negative about someone, say it verbally, not electronically. Remember that electronic communications can be sent from person to person, and are often not confined to the audience for which they are intended.

—⧆—

RULE #27:
Use e-mail to deal with individuals who place blame. If possible, include something in your e-mail that requires their reply.

I promised at the beginning of this book it would involve "positive politics." However, I also want to make you Teflon-coated from those who would harm you in the workplace, especially those who play the "blame game." Everybody in your organization knows who these people are. They are the ones who, as soon as things go wrong, start throwing people under the bus to deflect blame from themselves.

Here is how to deal with them: First, figure out who the blamers are. (It is usually not difficult; there are only a few people who are really good at it.) Next, quit writing CYA memos to everyone *except those few people*. Remember— every time you send a CYA memo to anyone it conveys the unspoken message, "I don't trust you." So the only people you ever *want* to get that kind of message from you are those few blamers whom you really do *not* trust!

When you have to work with one of these individuals, always follow up with an electronic memo that says essentially:

"Thanks so much for meeting with me yesterday. Just so I am clear and don't let anything fall between the cracks: I am going to do _____ and you are going to do_____."

Then, request at the end of your electronic memo that this individual send you some type of document. When you receive it, print off a copy of your memo and the document and put them in a file in your desk. If the project goes well, throw the documents away. If problems develop and the blamer starts blaming you, pull out the memo confirming what each person was supposed to do. If the person is an Olympic Blame-Placer, he will say he never got the memo. Then you can pull out the document you requested and say, "Really? Because here is the document you sent me in response to the memo." That will end the Blame-Placer Olympics.

Addendum to the rule—Do not "cc" anyone on your CYA memo. If you do, you will look weak, unable to handle the situation, and/or sneaky. You do not want to convey *any* of those things. Also, people get irritated when you clog their e-mail inbox with this stuff. You want people to really pay attention when you send them something. Do not devalue your electronic communication by needlessly burying people in it.

Another crucial point: Do not use your "blind copy" button except in very rare circumstances. When you get a blind copy of an electronic communication, you consciously or unconsciously say to yourself, "Well, if she's doing this to _____, I wonder how many times she's done it to me?" It only makes you look sneaky. If another person needs to be kept informed, simply copy him or her so everybody knows what is going on and everyone is in the loop.

RULE #28:
Never have an argument electronically . . . *especially* when you can prove you are right.

Nothing revs people up faster than seeing something negative about themselves in writing. So if you want to turn a common disagreement into a nuclear war, write and tell anyone how wrong they are. If you want a more positive outcome, go see the person—*especially* if you are absolutely convinced or can prove they are wrong. This will give them the opportunity to save face and change their mind without an audience following every step of their humiliation.

—◦◦◦—

RULE #29:
Re-check any e-mail or other electronic communication you send out at the end of the day, to guard against fatigue factor.

The quality of your work is always better the first couple of hours of your day than the last couple of hours (even if you are not a morning person). When you are trying to finish up a memo or empty your mailbox, you are focused on getting the work out, answering electronic communications, and not having to face those tasks the next morning. While I believe you should start your day with as little as possible left from the previous day, I suggest you execute that strategy a little differently. Try the following for 30 days: Do not send any e-mail or electronic communications of any substance the last hour or two of your workday. Instead, save them to your "Drafts" folder and make it standard practice to open that folder each morning right after you boot up your computer. No matter how short or long the communication is, you generally will edit at least one thing in it. This will make your first electronic communications of the day more diplomatic and persuasive.

—◦/◦/◦—

RULE #30:
Avoid using judgmental words in electronic communication.

Since the workplace is inhabited by flawed human beings, conflicts and harsh judgments are inevitable. You should *never* let the private opinions or judgments you might have of a fellow employee escalate to the point where you put those negative judgments in an electronic communication.

Don't get me wrong: I know this is sometimes easier said than done. Unfortunately, it is commonplace for one employee to bad-mouth another. Far too often, a manager will tell employees they have "an attitude problem"—a sure way to set the person off and make sure the entire discussion revolves around the manager's characterization of that person, rather than about addressing the person's performance. I am not saying the manager doesn't need to address these situations. I *am* saying the best way to fix these situations is to avoid using judgmental words in describing any person in the workplace, especially in an electronic communication or written document of any kind.

I once received a call from a client who told me a fellow manager had really done him dirty and planted the knife right between his shoulder blades. He told me he thought he needed to write an e-mail and send it to their mutual boss, to preserve the record of what had happened. I thought he was right. Because he was pretty upset (justifiably so), I suggested he send a draft to me before sending it to his boss. After editing the memo, I called him and said I assumed he wanted me to remove all the "wretched low-life" references from the memo. I also cautioned him against using "slithered" as a verb in any form of business correspondence. He and I both laughed and now, about once a year, he will send me something and ask me to "de-slither" it for him. Remember: Even if only seven percent of the meaning of your communication comes from the words you use, you still need to choose those words very carefully. Find someone in your life to "de-slither" any communication, especially electronic, if you are really upset when you write it.

———✺———

RULE #31:
Never use electronic communication
to blow off steam about someone at work or
about the workplace itself.

People treat electronic communication almost as if it were face-to-face conversation. Do not be lulled into this attitude. When you say something to your two most trusted friends in the break room, it evaporates into the air. If you say it electronically to those two friends, lots of people can have access to it. In addition, your two best friends may forward it to someone who holds the same opinion, but who is not nearly as trustworthy. So find someone at work to whom you can vent, but always do so in person, never in permanent print.

—◦◦◦—

RULE #32:
Electronic communication is professional correspondence. Make sure your spelling and grammar are always correct.

This is the rule I am most likely to violate. I have a wide vocabulary, but apparently am unable to spell half of what I can say. I am pleased to tell you that there has been a study done on bad spellers. This study concluded that bad spellers are missing an enzyme in their brains. I take great comfort in the fact that I am not stupid; I am just chemically imbalanced. Regardless, if this book were full of misspellings, you would immediately conclude, because you do not know me, that I am not smart or what I say has little value. When you get an electronic communication with mistakes Spell Check would have caught, you determine either that the person who sent it is not smart, is careless, or—worst of all—doesn't consider you important enough to check the work. Also—if you receive an electronic communication from me that contains errors such as misuse of "there" for "their" (which Spell Check will not catch), you automatically drop my IQ by at least 10 points. So make sure you proofread your work. Saving a draft and going back to it later, before sending it, will help you catch a lot of these mistakes.

Addendum to the rule—When employers have a great job to fill, they receive many resumes. Do not give a CEO, hiring manager, or recruiter the opportunity to throw out your resume because of spelling or grammatical errors. I know one CEO who says if there is a spelling or grammatical mistake *anywhere* on someone's cover letter or resume, that person is out of the running. The CEO told me, "This is the best work I'll ever see from them because they want this job. They could have had someone look at the resume for errors before they sent it. If this is their maximum effort, I don't need them!"

—⟶⟵—

RULE #33:
Avoid using certain abbreviations and symbols that are inappropriate for electronic business communications.

Do not use abbreviations like "LOL" or smiley-face symbols in your electronic business correspondence. If you have to tell me what emotion I should experience when I read your correspondence, it is not well crafted. Either re-draft it or come see me so I can get the rest of the meaning from your face and voice tone. If you are in doubt as to whether I will "get it" when you write it, there is a problem. If you say something I take as mean or sarcastic and then afterward say, "I was just joking," it will not fix the hurt I experienced when I read it. I will forgive you, but I will not forget how you made me feel.

Addendum to the rule—*Do not* use emoticons in your electronic business correspondence. While they are funny, I have a hard time respecting you as a professional when I get correspondence from you that has something winking at me!

Chapter Five

POLITICAL RULES ABOUT YOUR CO-WORKERS

I t is sad but true: Most of us spend more time with co-work-ers than with family members. But are we fully *developing* these relationships? Are we getting everything we *should* out of them? Are we doing the specific things necessary to make our work life go smoothly and make our co-workers *want* to go the extra mile for us? Just as with family mem-bers, you rarely get to choose your co-workers. So here are some rules for forging better relationships with co-workers and turning them into people who will watch your back and promote your career.

———◦◦◦———

RULE #34:
Always confront a co-worker in private.

If you disagree with a co-worker at a meeting, try not to do so in front of an audience. Nothing solidifies an individual's position faster than someone disagreeing with her in front of other people. You force her to act strong and make it impossible for her to change her mind and agree with your position. If you can, wait until after the meeting, go by her office, and tell her, "I didn't want to say this in the meeting, but I have a problem with one of your conclusions. I wanted to discuss it with you in private." She will appreciate your effort not to embarrass her and be much more receptive to your viewpoint.

If it is impossible to wait until after the meeting—if you are convinced her position is so wrong it will derail the entire meeting—try saying this, "Susie, I think when you made that decision (or came to that conclusion) there was a piece of information no one shared with you. That piece of information is…" and add an additional fact to the mix. By doing this, you alert Susie to the fact that you believe she has made a mistake, you give her a few minutes to think about her decision, and, most important, you give her room to change her mind and save face. She now can easily say, "Well, given that new information, I would decide things a little differently."

—◦◊◦—

RULE #35:
Go out of your way to help people when they are in trouble.

When co-workers make a public error—or everyone knows the boss is mad at them—it is a natural human tendency to avoid contact with them. They are often treated as if they are made of Kryptonite and everyone around them will be collateral damage if they get too close. The reality is, if they survive the incident (and in most cases they will), they will remember those who still talked to them and associated with them while they were working through the problem. If one of those people is *you*, you will have gained a loyal co-worker and an advocate for the life of your career. At worst, if they do *not* survive the incident, you are seen as someone who helps people and never kicks them when they are down—a good reputation to have in any organization.

—◦◊◦—

RULE #36:
Do not be unduly swayed by the opinions of the first person who offers to show you the ropes in a new situation. Get lots of feedback from many individuals.

Whenever you join a new organization or work situation, you have to assess your new situation as quickly as possible, so you can be as effective as possible as *fast* as possible. In all organizations or work groups, there are people who either do not fit in or are not plugged into what is going on. Sometimes it is both! I call these people "outlyers." Many times when someone new joins their organization or group, they are thrilled that they might finally have a friend and co-worker with whom they click. They will try to begin this relationship by "showing you the ropes." However, part of what makes them an outlyer is that, despite what they think, they are not plugged in and do not have a realistic view of what is going on in the group. Thank them for their insights, but do not act on them until you have checked them against the impressions of others in the group. One woman once confided to me that she lost her last job for this very reason. She said the two people her outlyer told her to be careful of were the two people with whom she should have built strong relationships.

You need to check anyone's advice with at least one other source before you act on it, especially in a new situation!

—∾∾—

RULE #37:
Do not be threatened by experts, but select and use them wisely.

At one time during my career, the CEO of my organization hired an outside consultant to help me with a project. I spent most of the project incensed that I did not get to select the consultant, and used every opportunity to point out his deficiencies. Essentially, I was re-fighting a war I already had lost. Instead, I should have befriended the consultant and used the situation as an opportunity to forge an alliance with him. At some point, the consultant was going to report back to the CEO informally, and I should have set myself and my department up to have positive things reported back.

I have on occasion been the consultant *inflicted* on a manager. I try very hard to be an advocate and make suggestions that will increase the manager's stock within his or her organization. I can remember following a director of human resources back to her office after a meeting and asking her how she thought the meeting had gone. I had been hired by the CEO to advise him about a particularly difficult personality issue that was brewing with one of the company's high-level, very valued senior executives. She was obviously not very happy to have me as a part of this issue and said, "I think the meeting went fine and I agree with what we have decided to do. But—no offense, Margaret—I could have told him what to do for free!"

I smiled and told her I understood her frustration, having been on the other side of this situation in the past, but went on to say, "Sometimes it is hard to be a prophet in your own land. Since you are stuck with me, why don't you tell me what your human resources agenda is? Perhaps I can help you sell it to the CEO and get additional support for some of the things you want to do. If you can't get rid of me, why don't you use me?" We became colleagues and good friends afterwards.

Having said that, whenever possible try to be the one who selects the consultants in the first place. That way, they will be loyal to you and will not criticize your efforts as a means of creating their next piece of business. Have an eyeball-to-eyeball conversation with consultants before they ever come on your premises and tell them, "I selected you for this project because I am looking for two results." Then describe the end result you want to achieve and add, "The second result I want is for you to look for opportunities and make suggestions about how my department could contribute more to the success of this organization. As you see those opportunities, I expect you to discuss them *only* with me. I am sure that if this works as I anticipate it will, we will have additional work for you in the future." This will keep the consultant from saying anything negative about your operation to anyone else in the organization. If the consultant does not immediately understand what you are saying, you need to re-think your selection.

—◦◦◦—

RULE #38:
Understand the alliances and animosities that exist within an organization. Try to avoid becoming involved in the animosities. Expect both to shift over time.

In your career, you will run into numerous people who operate on the premise that you are either "for me or against me," and who will expect you to choose a side. Simply because they are oriented that way does not mean you have to succumb to their way of thinking. Often, people will war back and forth in the workplace and try to involve you. They will constantly tell you negative things about someone else and then invite you to contribute your own negative stories on that individual. Resist the temptation, even if you agree with their assessment. You need to make as few enemies as possible in the workplace. Besides, you do not want to have a reputation for gossiping. Simply say to the person who wants to tell you a negative story, "Please don't tell me anything negative about _____. I have to work closely with him/her and it may make it difficult for me to do that." They have to stop telling you what they are dying to tell you because if they continue, they would be guilty of not caring whether they make your job more difficult. You also can say, "Really? That has not been my experience in working with _____." This may make them rethink their opinion of the individual.

Never get involved in other people's wars. They often make peace and then repeat everything negative others have said about their new ally.

RULE #39:
Remember that the negative feelings you instill in others can have a very long life in an organization.

I often ask participants in my politics seminars to think about the person in their career who has done them the dirtiest—the person who really planted the knife right between their shoulder blades. I then inquire about the timing of the event. For the thousands of people I have asked to participate in this exercise, the overwhelming majority have had the incident happen at least five or more years ago, with at least half saying the incident is more than ten years old. That is how long people's memories are concerning betrayal. You do not want to be stuck in anyone's mind like that—or for that long!

Chapter Six
POLITICAL RULES ABOUT YOUR BOSS

—⟶⟵—

RULE #40:
Stay neutral with new bosses.

When you get a new boss, you will be barraged by people asking you what you think of him/her. You would like to believe those questions reflect concern about your well-being. In some cases they do. However, in many cases, the people are looking for scandal, smut, and dirt. Be aware they will repeat what you say throughout the organization. So do not comment on your new boss to anyone. Simply say one of these two things: "He/she seems very smart, but I haven't worked with him/her for very long." Or: "He/she seems very nice, but I haven't worked with him/her for very long."

Either is noncommittal and positive. Keep saying one of these two things until people quit asking you how you like your new boss.

———◦∾◦———

RULE #41:
Align yourself with as many people as possible in your organization.

Never get sideways with anyone in your organization. Encourage your boss to do the same thing because your fortunes are tied to your boss' fortunes. You need your manager to be well-liked and respected. No matter how difficult the person you have to deal with is (especially if they are powerful), you must resist the temptation to square off against anyone simply because you do not (or your boss does not) like them. If your boss makes a negative comment about someone, try to nudge the situation by agreeing with your boss and then changing his or her focus. Or say this: "I know they are difficult, but we have to find a way to work with them, so we can be effective and accomplish our agenda." That is "stealth encouragement" to make your boss more politically savvy!

———◦∾◦———

RULE #42:
Never speak negatively about your boss. Any problems with his/her style should be discussed privately with your boss.

Never speak badly about your boss in the workplace—even if everyone else calls him "the Spawn of Satan." By not saying anything bad, you send several clear, positive, unspoken messages throughout your organization. The first is that you are loyal. This is particularly important when other managers in your organization (who may have the next great job you want) observe your behavior. The second unspoken message you send is that you are tough and resilient. And the third unspoken message is that you can work for anyone. All these qualities are great ones for your organization to believe you possess. You enhance your value and reputation—simply by shutting up.

——✦——

RULE #43:
Do not compare yourself to others when discussing your career with your boss. Justify your request for a raise or promotion based upon merit and not time in the position. Avoid having this discussion immediately following a compliment from your boss.

Never say "How come Joe/Susie gets _____?" It makes you look petty and clueless. It is perfectly acceptable to say, "I would like to serve on the next special project." Or: "I would like to be promoted into management." Or: "I would like to make more money. What do I need to start doing to make that happen?" It is professional and tells the individual with whom you are speaking that you want to be treated like Joe/Susie (who seem to be getting more perks than you are). It also shows you are willing to do what you need to do to earn your perks.

Learn to accept a compliment without making your boss feel you are always looking for a moment of weakness to get something additional for yourself. When your boss says something nice about you, do not deflect the compliment with modesty or humor by cracking the old joke about "Maybe this is a good time to ask for a raise." This devalues the compliment and creates an awkward situation for everyone present, even if they know you are kidding. Here is the perfect reply: "Thank you so much. That means a great deal to me coming from you." You now have tripled the chances your boss will say more nice things about you in the future.

─────

RULE #44:
Maintain an ongoing dialogue with other departments, the corporate office, and/or your governing body.

If you have a corporate office and/or governing body, it is very easy to have negative feelings about them and criticize them. If you are in a business unit or department, the one thing *everyone* agrees on is how stupid/out-of-touch the corporate office/governing body is regarding what it is like to be on the firing lines, having to execute some of the _____ (fill in the most common negative adjective you hear) directives from them. One of the bigger political mistakes I made when I worked for companies that were part of multi-company conglomerates was to build relationships with my counterparts in the other companies by bemoaning our common enemy—THE CORPORATE OFFICE! The one thing we had in common was our desire to tell stories about all the dumb things CORPORATE made us do! This game was especially entertaining at the bar one night, at the end of a long day, during a conference sponsored by CORPORATE! It finally dawned on me that I was taking potshots at the very people who determined what benefits my employees would get . . . and who determined *executive compensation*, in other words, what *I* got paid! It was fun and satisfying—but "career stupid."

This rule also applies to any other department in your organization. I know for a fact that if you criticized Human Resources (my department), we always heard about it. Remember, we are the department that can slow walk your hiring paperwork, raises, etc., but never appear to do so. We also can do something to your vacation accrual from which you may never recover!

A special aside to those of you *in* the corporate office, governing body, or other departments about being politically astute. You need the people in the field to execute whatever plan has been devised and you need to listen to them about the best way to execute it. Otherwise, they do just enough to be in compliance, but will not anticipate or mention problems they can clearly see at the onset. Many times they will secretly let the plan fail because no one wanted their input on planning the project. If you *truly* want to be my "partner," ask me *what*

I need to run my business, rather than, "Here's what we're providing." Assume *no one* knows more about what I need—or has a greater vested interest in what will really work and make my department/organization successful—than I do. After all, my job depends upon my department/organization being successful. In addition, consider *not* homogenizing what you do for every organization within your reach because many operations have different cultures, functions, employee demographics, etc. What works for one does not always work for another. If it makes sense to homogenize, show each entity how it is an advantage to *them,* not how much it works for the corporate office. This keeps business units and subsidiaries from resenting what they pay in corporate overhead and/or salaries. One person who attended one of my seminars had worked in the corporate office and then had moved to one of the business units. She stated it pretty succinctly when she said, "I have deployed stuff and I have been deployed upon."

———*◦◦◦*———

Political Assignments to Enhance Your Career

At the beginning of the Political Rules, your assignment was to circle the rule in each chapter that you are *most* likely to violate. You now should have six circled. Pick two out of the six and begin working on them today.

Often when I speak on the topic of positive office politics, someone will say, "I think I knew all these rules." When I ask how they have changed their behavior because they were aware of the rules, they confess they have not. So despite knowing they should not be doing certain things, they still do them. Their rationale can be anything from "I just forget in the heat of the moment" to "You have no idea how awful _____ is to deal with." What this *really* means is this individual has a lot of knowledge, but no application. Application is the only thing that counts. It is not how smart are you, but what you *do* with it.

Once you have selected the two rules—and corrected your behavior with regard to those two rules—tackle two more. And then two more—until you have worked your way through the entire list of 44 rules. At that point, you should be seen as a mover and shaker in your organization and will be as fire-proof as anyone can be in this day.

One other Political Assignment: Look at the six rules you initially circled. Do they have anything in common? Do you violate them in certain situations? Does a specific person make you violate them? Learn to recognize these situations so you become especially adept at not violating the rules.

Here is a true story that illustrates how this process will help you:

I once worked with a very smart female executive, who could not seem to keep anyone working for her long-term. Her people skills were poor. So I was tasked to help her work on those skills as this constant churn of people was limiting her effectiveness. I noticed that often—right before she said something harsh to one of her employees—she would say, "I absolutely disagree with you." What usually came after that was pretty brutal. I pointed out the behavior to her, and we agreed that when she *heard* those words come out of her mouth, she absolutely would *not* say what she had planned to say next. She would simply close her mouth, no matter how silly it made her look, in order to avoid the behavior that was causing her problems. Then we worked on hearing those words in her head before she ever even said them. Soon, she progressed to the strategy for saying "no" without actually saying "no." (See Rule #1—Learn to say "yes" if at all possible.)

Chapter Seven

HOW TO TELL WHO HAS *REAL* POWER AND INFLUENCE

I wrote earlier about the need to build a wide network of supporters to advance your career, as well as to support you when you make a mistake. Not only is it important to have a large network, it is even more important to have *powerful people* in your network. In organizations today, not everyone's vote counts...and some people have more than one vote!

Never confuse title with power. There are people in organizations who have senior titles, but who are not particularly powerful. They are very competent at the function they have been asked to perform, but they are not really movers and shakers in their organizations. The converse also is true:

THE HIDDEN LANGUAGE OF BUSINESS

Some people who have unimpressive titles wield great power. I once worked for a CEO whose administrative assistant was very powerful. I watched her break several individuals' careers and they never knew what hit them. If she did not like you, she would say negative things about you to the CEO. Within 30 days, I would begin to hear the CEO say those same things about the individual she did not like. If you wanted to see the CEO and she liked you, you simply had to ask for an appointment with the CEO and she would get you in to see him that day. If she did not like you, she would tell you it would be three days before she could get you on his appointment calendar. She was a very bitter and mean human being.

As head of human resources for the company, I was asked by my group if I was going to address this with the CEO. They felt that, because I had a good relationship with him, he might listen to me. While I have never shied away from handling tough situations, I know that being politically astute means picking your battles and recognizing a no-win situation before you step into it. I reminded them that she drafted almost all the replies to his correspondence even before he saw it. She fended off people he did not want to talk to and knew who should be put through to him immediately. She made all his travel arrangements and made sure he was upgraded to first class. When I pointed these things out to the people in HR, I posed the question: "Do you think he would really want me to bring this up? He is not going to fire her and I will put him in the awkward position of appearing weak. No, what we are going to do is pursue a good relationship with her and do what we have to do to make her like and respect our department. Also, we are going to help people who have come within her sights to dodge her wrath, if at all possible. That way, we will not get sideways with the CEO and maybe we will be able to blunt her negative effect on the workplace. It was one of the hardest things we ever had to do.

In the next few pages, I am going to give you 11 subtle ways to tell who has power and influence in an organization. Watch for these cues so you will be able to identify the real power brokers in any organization:

—◦◦◦—

POWER SIGNAL #1:
Complete "catch up" is done for them if they join a meeting late.

Watch what happens when someone joins a meeting late. If the meeting stops for a few moments when the person walks in and someone says, "Where we are is…" and then gives a quick synopsis of what has been happened so far, you are probably looking at someone who is powerful. If you are not particularly powerful, the group accepts your apology for being late, you slide into your seat, and you have to catch yourself up as the penalty for being late. What the group is really reacting to is that if this powerful person is not on board, whatever they are meeting about probably has little chance of succeeding.

—◦◦◦—

POWER SIGNAL #2:
They suffer no penalty for habitually showing up late to meetings.

No matter how rude and arrogant this may seem, it is a sure sign someone is powerful. While people may comment or joke about the fact that they always run late, no one is willing to come down on them hard enough to make them observe the social niceties we expect from others. It may not be right, but it is real, and complaining about it only erodes your credibility, not theirs.

—◦◦◦—

POWER SIGNAL #3:
When they speak, everyone stops talking.

Watch carefully for these people in meetings. No matter how many people are talking or how heated the discussion gets when they offer an opinion, everyone stops talking to listen to what this individual has to say. You can cultivate this reputation by rarely speaking in meetings and thereby giving great weight to the few opinions you express.

Addendum to the rule—On those few occasions when you do speak, make sure you sound strong and sure. Some people do not speak because they are timid. Or when they do weigh in, they speak so softly they sound meek. Be very careful not to trail off at the end of your point or allow your tone to rise at the end of a sentence. These mannerisms give the impression you are unsure. Also, do not lead your points with questions such as "Don't you think we should…?" Or, "Wouldn't it be a good idea if we…?" If you do, you will be seen as asking permission or seeking approval. Rather, say, "I think we should…." If others disagree with you, that is okay. It is not okay if they think you are weak or timid!

—◦◦◦—

POWER SIGNAL #4:
They are able to operate outside the normal organizational restraints.

This one will make most people rant and rave. And there are many examples of it: Perhaps there is a hiring freeze on and suddenly a manager gets to replace someone or—even more aggravating—the manager gets an increase in head count. Or another example: You have been told not to make any more capital expenditures this fiscal year, and suddenly someone gets new equipment or funding for a new sales or marketing campaign. If you have asked those above you why this is being permitted and you do not get a good, clear answer, *stop asking!* Do the people you are asking understand this goes against the rules everyone else has to follow? Yes. Are they any happier about it than you are? Probably not, but they do understand that these people are powerful enough to shake the corporate tree and get what they need. Railing about it only makes you unpopular with senior managers who have already signed off on this course of action.

One of the most astute mentors I have ever had, Nick Jordan (I still go to him for advice 20 years later), gave me a political lesson I will never forget. We had a peer, the vice president of marketing, who was incredibly creative but equally arrogant. He ignored requests from other departments, but constantly got additional resources and increases in head count when no one else got them. I often complained to my boss, the CEO, about this. The CEO always said he would deal with the situation, but nothing seemed to change. Nick was a fellow VP and asked me one day what I knew about the CEO and this VP of marketing's history. I told him I knew they had worked together once before at a different company. My mentor then informed me they had worked together two other times in the past. Every time the CEO changed companies, he recruited this VP of marketing to come work for him. So here was my profound lesson: My mentor looked me squarely in the eye and simply said, "Margaret, stop smacking the teacher's pet!"

POWER SIGNAL #5:
People say, "How are we going to sell [person's name] on this?"

Listen to the name that gets filled in that blank and the tone with which it is said. If the tone conveys concern or fear, you are looking at someone who is powerful. People know this endeavor is destined to fail if that person does not support it or chooses to actively block it. Also listen for this: "Susie's not going to like this." If that is expressed with concern or a negative shake of the head, you know Susie is powerful. If the tone seems to have a smile to it and an attitude of "I cannot wait to see the fit she throws when she hears this," you know Susie is not particularly powerful.

―――∕∕∕∕―――

POWER SIGNAL #6:
People who work for them get higher raises than are normal in your organization.

While no one should ever discuss the amount of money they receive for a raise, the reality is everyone talks. Everyone knows who the managers are who seem to get more money for their people. It may come in the form of a larger annual increase than normal or in their ability to get their people promoted either legitimately or through a faux promotion (an elevation in title but no real change in job duties) in order to pay them more money.

―――∕∕∕∕―――

POWER SIGNAL #7:
They can disregard requests from other business units and not suffer any long-term, adverse consequences.

They never turn in their budgets, performance reviews, succession plans, etc., on time, but nothing ever happens to them. They can ignore e-mails from other departments, never answer them, and yet they continue to prosper. This is some-one who is a powerful contributor in some aspect; someone who is so important to the organization that no one is willing to really penalize them for this lack of responsiveness. Chances are they come through when the organization needs them in such a spectacular way that their unresponsive behavior pales in comparison to what they deliver.

—◦◦◦—

POWER SIGNAL #8:
When a crisis arises, your CEO (or the highest level person in your organization) meets with them behind closed doors.

Pay attention to whom the highest-level person in your organization turns when they have to make a crucial decision. You will not be privy to those discussions, nor will they take place in a regular meeting, but pay attention to the identity of the individual who has that one-on-one meeting with the CEO. If you have watched any of *The Godfather* movies, this is the equivalent of the consigliore—the person whose advice and counsel carries great weight in the organization. You need to know who that person is.

—◦/◦/◦—

POWER SIGNAL #9:
Their areas routinely suffer fewer budget cuts than other areas.

Regardless of what organization you are a part of, the budgeting process is pretty much the same. Everyone gets instructions in a budget packet (memo, guidelines—whatever this is called in your organization) and they do their budgets. They then are sent to the finance department for someone to combine and roll up into the next year's budget. If they collectively come in too high, they are returned to everyone with instructions to cut them by X percent. If they still do not get reduced far enough, someone meets with each manager or department head and helps them individually cut their budget until they are in line with what the next year's revenues (or budget dollars) and expenses need to be. In these budget wars, powerful people lose fewer dollars as a percent of their overall budget than other departments do.

Early on in my career, I worked with a CFO who thought my department was a huge waste of money. As a matter of fact, he said openly in a meeting that he thought we could eliminate my department and never miss a beat. We were under terrible budget constraints one year and no one could get his or her budget down far enough without making drastic cuts. If my department took too great a hit, I was going to have to lay off one or two of the eight people working in my area.

We had reached the point where each vice president had

to meet with the CFO and CEO individually to pare down their budgets. It was a pretty big bloodbath, with people losing thousands of dollars in these meetings. My meeting with the CEO and CFO was scheduled after lunch one afternoon. The CFO came to my office that morning, rubbing his hands together and telling me I needed to decide who was getting laid off because my department was going to be half the size it was now, once he was done with my budget.

Now, my CEO was a great supporter of the things we were doing, but the money had to come from somewhere and the CFO was clearly gunning for my department. Since I felt there was no way I could win the CFO over, I figured I would need a strong ally in the CEO. I knew the CEO had a great sense of humor and I thought if I could make him laugh, I might come through the meeting with my department intact. I arrived for the meeting with all my backup detail and stacks of papers. I had hardly taken a seat before the CFO suggested that we start with my head count. At that point I told both men, "Before we get started, I have brought a visual aid to assist me in my budget presentation." I pulled what looked like a malformed apple out of a bag and put it in the middle of the conference table. My CEO fell out of his chair laughing, and the CFO got red in the face and asked, "What is that and why is this so funny?" My CEO looked at him and said, "Joe, it's a turnip. As in 'you can't get blood out of one!'" My meeting was the shortest of all the six VPs and I only lost $10,000, which meant no reduction in head count. Being politically savvy means reading your audience well, understanding who can be converted to your cause, and how to convert them.

Here is the negative political lesson I learned from that situation: I came in the next morning to find the turnip sitting in the middle of my desk with my letter opener stuck completely through it. Ketchup was bleeding from it and all the way across the surface of my desk. When the CFO arrived that morning, he stood in my doorway and told me I was so lucky—but he would be ready for me the next year! I left the company before the next year's budget had to be finalized, making my own head the head-count reduction.

—◦◦◦—

POWER SIGNAL #10:
As the organization changes, they are able to maintain their position or move up.

As organizations change, watch the people who lose responsibilities and those who gain them. If an individual is able to move up, especially when the organization is going through budget cuts or a significant change in senior management, you are looking at someone who understands how to thrive within any power structure. If they do it more than once or survive more than one regime change, they are exceptionally powerful.

Also, you should watch for what I call the "Three Card Monty Power Grab." This is an individual who manages to trade a relatively low-level responsibility for an extremely important one, all the while saying they just changed responsibilities and their job is really no different from anyone else's.

—⟶⟍⟍⟍⟶—

POWER SIGNAL #11:
They deliver results.

The fastest way I know to become a powerful person in your organization is to "over-deliver" results. When you deliver phenomenal results, no one questions why you need additional resources and no one questions your methods. They are happy to give them to you because they know the investment will come back to the organization two-, three- or four-fold. No one will look over your shoulder as long as you keep delivering.

It is crucial politically that you understand what delivering results means to your organization. It is not always what you think. Often compliance functions—like human resources, the finance department, or the legal department—believe it means keeping your organization out of trouble. It does mean that, but not if your organization loses its flexibility to grow and respond to marketplace needs. If you are constantly saying "no" (See Rule #1—Learn To Say "Yes" If At All Possible), you are not delivering sufficient results.

Why is it important to know who has power and influence? Because not only do you want to make sure you do not get sideways with any of them (because they make career-ending enemies), you also want these people to be proponents and supporters of yours. You need them as a part of your network.

———◦◦◦———

Political Assignments to Enhance Your Career

Take a few minutes to review the 11 ways to tell who has power and influence. Make a list of those people in your current organization who have *real* power and influence. Over the next year, plan how you will get to know each one better. Either serve on a committee of which each is a member or volunteer for a project that will get you exposure to them. You want them to know who you are, to appreciate the caliber of your work, and to say nice things about you throughout your organization.

Chapter Eight

FORGING A BETTER RELATIONSHIP WITH YOUR MANAGER

One of the most important political alliances to cultivate is your relationship with your boss. Start by asking yourself this question: "Do I actually *manage* my relationship with my boss . . . or just try not to make him/ her mad?" Most people do *only* the latter. Turn that around and start creating a more positive, effective relationship with your boss by answering these key questions:

—◦◦◦—

BOSS QUESTION #1:
What is the method of communication with which my boss is most comfortable?

Is it face-to-face, e-mail, voicemail, or formal meeting? I had a boss who responded best to voicemail. He wasn't big on face-to-face because it required too much time. He could return five voicemails in airports faster than he could type e-mails on his PDA. If you voicemailed him, you almost always got an answer the same day, even when he was busy. This strategy also made me look very self-sufficient because I wasn't always in his office asking questions. On the rare occasion when I asked for time on his calendar, he would move me to the head of the line because he knew it was important.

—◦◦◦—

BOSS QUESTION #2:
How does my boss like to receive information?

Does your boss like you to lay out the problem so she can make a decision or does she expect you to suggest a solution? Does she want the facts and then time to think about the solution? If so, you do not want to bring her an issue and then immediately ask her what she wants to do about it. You want to lay the situation out and then say, "I don't need an answer immediately. Tomorrow is fine." or "We don't have to decide today. I just wanted to give you a heads up."

Also, in what order does your boss like to get information? This is especially important if you are building a report for her. Does she want the issue and then the answer with the backup detail attached? Or does she want the issue, all the variables you considered, the analysis you went through, and then the conclusion? If you stack the report incorrectly, you run the risk of your boss either thinking you are slow-thinking, slow-moving, or that you shoot from the hip and are not careful and precise in your decision-making.

—————

BOSS QUESTION #3:
During what time of day is my boss most receptive to talking?

Your boss may be a morning person or more open to longer conversations as the day winds down and the phones stop ringing. Is your boss more amenable after lunch than before? If your boss is talkative and you need a *quick* answer, check their calendar or understand their lunch schedule and go see them 15 minutes before they have a meeting or before they typically leave for lunch.

I am not a morning person, nor am I a coffee drinker. I drink hot tea, which has plenty of caffeine as well. I am not worth much without at least one cup of tea in the morning. I once overheard Tanya Bowker, one of the support people in my department, tell a manager who was on the way to see me at 8:01 a.m., "She's in, but if you are going to ask her for something, I'd come back in about 20 minutes. She just made her tea!" To tell you how savvy Tanya really was . . . I remember coming in one morning and unlocking my door. I sensed someone behind me and there was Tanya with a steaming cup of tea for me. She said, "Put down your briefcase and take a big slug of tea because this situation won't wait!" Tanya was one of the most politically savvy and effective people I ever worked with, and everyone was constantly trying to recruit her to their department.

—◦◦◦—

BOSS QUESTION #4:
On what day of the week is my boss most receptive to talking?

Is there a particular day of the week that is better for your boss than others? I asked this question in a seminar for a mixture of managers and supervisors from different parts of a county government. In the session, I happened to have one of the Directors and five of his direct reports. When we discussed this question, one of his direct reports immediately responded, "Oh that's an easy one—Wednesday mornings! Our boss has his weekly meeting with the Commissioners on Tuesday afternoon. He spends all day Monday and Tuesday morning getting prepared. He's wound so tight that we try not to talk to him at all. And he's so relieved on Wednesday morning that we can get just about anything out of him!" I told her I thought her analysis was excellent, but that I would not have shared that observation with my boss in the room!

＝◆◇◆＝

BOSS QUESTION #5:
What are the three most important things to my boss?

When you answer this question about your manager, be sure to focus on both work and non-work-related items. This is the key to understand their value system—the system by which everything gets measured. Does your boss want everybody to be happy? Then present your plan as the one that works for the most people. If your boss is simply bottom-line driven, then do your homework and show your manager how much money your idea makes or saves the organization. If your manager is very family-oriented, present ideas in terms of making jobs easier and/or providing work/life balance for your employees. If their focus is community service, present your idea in terms of enhancing your organization's image in the community. You will be more successful if you speak to your manager's value system at the same time you present your agenda.

＝◆◇◆＝

BOSS QUESTION #6:
What are my boss's top three business concerns?

Over a casual lunch with your manager one day, ask him, "What are the top three things about our department/ organization that keep you up at night?" Do not comment or try to make him feel as though it may not be as bad as he believes. Just listen. You are not trying to allay his concerns, but to understand what is causing his stress at work. Spend some time (days or weeks, not hours) thinking about the things he shared with you and what you could do to impact them positively in some way. Any suggestion you make sends several unspoken positive messages about you to your boss: It tells him you are focused on the things that count (at least in his mind) . . . that you care about making his job easier . . . and that you are a big-picture, strategic thinker.

—————

BOSS QUESTION #7:
What are the top three irritants for my boss at work?

What pushes your manager's hot buttons? You need to really think about this because if you keep stomping on those things, your relationship will never go well. You will simply be tolerated, not valued, which is not a good relationship to have with any manager.

One of my top irritants is the person who says, "That's not in my job description." There is nothing wrong with people who want to be clear about their job duties, but those who over-do it are going to struggle working for me. Tanya, whom I spoke about earlier in this chapter, was a master at spotting people's hot buttons. I once gave her an assignment that was way out of her comfort level. She was smart enough not to show any hesitation, but simply said, "I can't wait to learn how to do this. Where can I go to get more information so I do a great job for you?"

Kayla Barrett, one of the consultants with whom I work, tells a story about her manager, the COO, who had a standing meeting on Monday morning for a status update on a huge, highly visible project she was managing for him. Because she is extremely social and builds her network through relationships, she always would ask how his weekend had gone. He would answer, but over time she realized he would prefer to get straight to the matter at hand. So she became more task-focused and began each meeting with a status update on the project—nothing more. Over time, they developed a very good working relationship and he began to ask her how her weekend had been. Even today, he hires her repeatedly for outside consulting assignments because she requires little instruction, gets to the point, and never wastes his time.

—⟨∞⟩—

BOSS QUESTION #8:
When my boss needs advice, with whom does he/she consult?

Think of this advisor as your boss' "consigliere." Build a good relationship with this person so he/she says good things about you to your boss. Remember—this is someone to whom your boss listens and whose opinion your boss greatly values.

—⟨◦/◦/◦⟩—

BOSS QUESTION #9 (Optional):
What are the last three business books my boss has read?

Any book your manager spends his/her valuable time reading, you should read. I know one manager who wanted funding in the budget for an additional person, but knew his boss hated any increase in head count. His boss was a great fan of the book *Good to Great*. Even though the manager was not a big reader, he read the book because his boss so valued its insights. The manager then justified his request for the new position by saying he needed "the right people on the bus in the right seats" (wording that comes straight from *Good to Great*). This resonated with his boss and he got the okay to hire the new person.

You also can be politically savvy by giving your boss the gift of a business book you have recently read and with which you agree. (Not this book or you will give away all your secrets!) This allows you to use the author as an expert to convert your boss to your way of thinking. Be sure to inscribe the book on the inside flyleaf and sign your name. That way, every time they open the book, they are reminded of the gift. If they lend it to someone, you will appear to be smart, cutting edge, and someone whose opinion your boss values because they read your suggestions.

If your boss is not a reader, you still can use this strategy. Select a book that is short but packed with insights, so your boss will be willing to spend an hour or so reading it. *Never* put the cost of the book on your expense report. This is a gift—and an investment in your career. Surely your career is worth $20 or $25!

——————

Political Assignments to Enhance Your Career

Really work through these nine "Boss Questions." Do not just think about them; write your answers down. Then commit to three concrete ways you are going to change your behavior with your current manager. See if your annual performance appraisal is not better next year because of these changes!

SELECTING A
CAREER MENTOR

No matter how smart you are, how much experience
you have, or how talented you are, you need a *great*
career mentor. It is impossible for any person to
view himself, his decisions, or his actions dispassionately.
We cannot see ourselves as others see us, understand what
impression our actions may leave on others, or identify what
a career mistake is until sometimes long after we have made
it…if *then*! A really great career mentor can help you with
all these things, and point out behavior patterns that are
destructive for you long-term.

Neither your manager nor anyone in your chain-of-
command can serve this role for you. They can coach you
to make you a better performer, but they cannot mentor
you. The role of a true mentor is that of a confidant, teacher,

and judge all in one. They must be a person with whom you can discuss your mistakes and shortcomings with no fear it will come back to haunt you on a performance review or limit your opportunities in the succession planning of your organization. For this reason, you need to look beyond your chain-of-command for your career mentor.

Do not pick someone simply because you like her or get along well with him. This individual needs to be able to tell you when you have "screwed up," even when your intentions were noble. He/she needs to tell you when you are in trouble in your organization—and even when you need to update your resume and move on. You need someone who is savvy enough to teach you something, tough enough to hold your feet to the fire regarding executing what you have agreed to do, and frank enough to tell you the honest truth.

Here is a very methodical, deliberate way to select your career mentor:

First, make a list of 10 individuals in the work world today whom you believe are smart, savvy, and very honest. You must have some sort of connection with each of these individuals. That connection must be sufficient enough that you could get each to take your telephone call. However, you need not know each of them well. For instance, the person could be someone you heard speak at a conference (not a celebrity speaker, but perhaps a local one). Or the person can be from your organization, but work in an entirely different area. For instance, if you are in sales, you could select a mentor from operations or finance. In fact, I encourage you to think about selecting someone who does *not* do what you do, so you get a different perspective as you discuss your career.

Once you have created your list, rank those 10 names from one to ten, starting with the person with whom you would be most comfortable discussing all your "bumps and warts." Then determine how much mentoring time you need over the next year. Here is a hint: Remember that really great mentors are busy. The most you should ask for is an hour a month. If this person is extremely good, that will be an invaluable hour.

Next, call the top person on your list to ask him/her to be your mentor. Be very upfront about what you want and get to the point quickly. These people are busy and you do not want them to believe that mentoring you will be a hassle or overly time-consuming. I suggest a conversation that goes something like this:

"Mr. Smith, I am _____. I had the pleasure of hearing you speak at the Chamber of Commerce meeting last week. I thought what you said was insightful, as well as thought-provoking and cutting edge. I am looking for someone like you to mentor me *for the next year*. I will need no more than an hour per month and wondered if I might impose on you to help me."

This is one of the most flattering, compelling phone calls anyone can receive. If he says "yes," immediately thank him heartily, because he has just consented to help you in a big way. Then quickly tell him you will do this in whatever way is most convenient for him. Offer to buy his dinner, lunch, breakfast, or coffee once a month, and tell him you will come prepared with questions and situations about which you wish to ask for guidance. If that is too much for him, ask if you can do this by phone, by setting up a monthly telephone conversation. The best outcome is if he agrees to dinner. People rarely have dinner in a restaurant for just an hour, so you will get more than an hour per month of his time. *Do not* let him pay for dinner. This is an investment in your career and worth more than dinner could ever cost you. If you have a limited budget, scout out interesting, inexpensive places and invite him there. Be sure to pick a place quiet enough for easy conversation.

If he says "no," you have lost nothing. He still will be flattered—and unlikely to forget you in the future. Someday you may be able to use that telephone call as a jumping-off point for a future opportunity.

I have had the same mentor for almost 20 years. He was a VP of sales for a company where I was hired to be the new VP of human resources, about five jobs ago for me. When I met him during the interview process, I was impressed with how he handled himself and how insightful his answers to my questions were. I also knew he had worked for the CEO in a previous job. I went to him shortly after I started work because I perceived there were a lot of different factions in the organization and there were several tugs of war going on behind the scenes. I told him that—while I brought years of experience in human resources to this job—I knew that how you begin a job could determine how successful you would be long-term. I then said, "Every organization has its hidden land mines and unspoken taboos. I would really appreciate it if you could keep me from losing a professional limb my first 60 to 90 days on the job until I figure out where the political

WORKPLACE POLITICS, POWER & INFLUENCE

land mines are located." He laughed, said he understood what I meant, and would be glad to help. Today, our mentoring sessions go quickly because he knows me so well (my strengths *and* weaknesses) and we cut to the chase rapidly. Just so you know he is not afraid to tell me the unvarnished truth, see my story about "not smacking the teacher's pet" in the chapter "How to Tell Who Has *Real* Power and Influence." You need a mentor who is that honest.

Sometimes you will start with a mentor who is helpful in your early career, but whom you outgrow as you advance. I see this happen when the mentor retires (not always, but sometimes). Your mentor may be out of the work force for awhile and does not keep up with changes in the work world. So you may have to repeat your mentor search later in your career. If you outgrow your mentor more than twice, particularly within a few years, you need to question your selection list. You should select well enough to have your mentor for a decade (or the rest of your career if you are lucky!), so you get better and better advice as the person gets to know you better.

Some *rare* individuals may need *two* mentors because of the paths their careers have taken. I have another mentor, besides the one I described above. He became a mentor to me late in my career, when I transitioned to owning my own business. His name is Jim Clayton and I taught my first management class as a consultant for his management group. He gave me numerous references my first year in business. I am pleased to say he is still a client today and he is the person I go to when I need advice about pricing and marketing for my business. He has a particular expertise in Sales and Marketing and pushes me to increase prices when I am convinced no one will pay a higher rate. He is always right . . . and always asks for a deal when he books me!

Addendum to the rule—I suggested you use a one-year time frame when you first approach your prospective mentor. At the end of 12 months, *do not* call your mentor and ask if he/she will "re-up" for another 12 months. Just keep calling and taking him/her to dinner until he/she tells you to stop. Most will never want to stop. If they do, you need to look at whether you are (1) wearing them out with questions; (2) depending on them to hold your hand instead of advise you; or (3) ignoring their advice so often they conclude they are wasting their time.

—◦◦◦—

Political Assignment to Enhance Your Career

Lock down a really great career mentor in the next month and get started. Do not wait six months to complete this assignment. You understand the mentor-selection process now, and you are never too busy for good advice and counsel.

Chapter Ten
CAREER PLANNING

Performance is the price of admission to be promoted.
—Harvey Coleman,
author of *Empowering Yourself*

Whether you want to eventually be at the highest level of an organization—or simply do meaningful, fulfilling work—you need a strategic career plan. If you do not have one, you likely will drift, and look back on a half-century of work with regrets that you did not make more things—or different things—happen for yourself. You need to be constantly improving your skill set and honing your talents, so you have lots of choices along the way. This means you have to plug the holes in your skill sets and step outside your comfort zone. In some cases, you will even need to step outside your chosen profession. You can do this by working through three specific questions about your work life to this point. These questions enable you to see where the holes are in your development so you can plan to fill those voids. The more you know and can do, the more choices you will have regarding the nature and quality of your work. This means you will have to develop new skills and talents, some of which you may dislike. Later in your career you will be grateful you explored those skills because doing so will teach you which types of work to pursue, and which to avoid.

Begin by taking stock of the current skill sets you have. Ask yourself this question:

—◦◦◦—

"What are the skills and talents I currently possess?"

In other words, what do you already know how to do, including soft talents and skills? In my case, the list would be the one presented below. You will see, in the parenthetical information following each skill, how I managed to acquire each skill or talent:

- Interview and hire employees (25 years of human resources experience)
- Negotiate a union contract (worked for a company that had union and non-union facilities)
- Defend and prosecute a lawsuit (five years of practice as a trial lawyer)

- Draft a contract (B+ in my Contracts course in law school)
- Run a 24/7 call-center operation (volunteered to run operations while a search was launched for a new VP of operations)
- Make a sales call (volunteered to travel all over the U.S. during a new product launch to sell the new product to existing and prospective clients)
- Develop a marketing plan (nine years of owning my own business)
- Develop a seminar or training program (12 years as a management consultant, four years before that for my last employer)
- Create a PowerPoint presentation (one-day seminar and painful trial and error)
- Write a book (my first book, *Management Courage—Having the Heart of a Lion*, was published in 2006)
- Make a speech (lots of practice and preparation, as well as teaching numerous seminars)
- Oversee facilities maintenance (volunteered to be responsible for this when my last company was bought from our parent company. I hired Corporate's best maintenance guy, promising him he could run his own shop and pick his own people if he would teach me what I needed to know along the way. Thank you, Tony Hodges, for all I know about heating, wiring, sprinkler systems, safety, and emergency response!)

- Teach managers and their employees to work together without third-party interventions (being a middle child plus 30 years of management and human resources experience).

While this is not the whole list, it is a large part of it. You need to make your own *candid* list. It should only include those skills and talents that are transferable from organization to organization because this becomes your "walking skill set"— talents you can use for multiple employers.

The next question to ask yourself is:

"What are the general business areas in which I have experience?"

For me, it is these four:
Human Resources
Operations
Legal
Sales/Marketing
And the final question to ask yourself is:

"For my current employer, what are the departments in which I have worked?"

This question is great for determining whether you are stagnating in your current position and whether your current organization offers opportunities for you to stretch and grow.

Once you have answered these three questions—created these three lists—the weaknesses or holes in your knowledge base become apparent. For example, based on what little information I gave you, it is obvious I am weak in finance and technology. I like people much more than I do machines or numbers—and it shows! But that limited me in my career. So I shored up my weakness in finance by taking a course entitled "Finance for Non-Financial Managers." I still read constantly about finance and take short seminars and courses to keep up with its rapid changes. I do not have the luxury of saying, "I do not need to know that" or "I cannot learn to do that."

You do not necessarily have to take a course to shore up your weak spots. You also can look for opportunities to serve on committees or project teams that broaden your experience within your organization or you can fill in for a job in a different department while someone is on a leave of absence. You can even volunteer to take a piece of a job while your organization is searching for a replacement. The more you know—the more skills you develop—the more choices you have to create the future you want, rather than merely the future your organization determines for you. Constantly enhancing your skills makes you a more valuable employee, less likely to be laid off, and more employable when looking for a new position.

—◦◦◦—

Political Assignment to Enhance Your Career

Make those three lists within the next 30 days and commit to acquiring one new skill or talent in the next 12 months.

CONCLUSION

I encourage you to become politically astute in your organization and in other organizations with which you come in contact. Do the exercises suggested in this book. Do not sit back and tell yourself you are not going to "play politics" because, if you do, you will have wasted your potential. You will never rise as high in an organization as you could have, never be able to influence a decision for the better, and never be the best manager for the people who work for you. You need positive political power and a network of allies who will support you . . . or at least who will not undermine your efforts. Office politics only become dirty when people have self-serving motives, or revenge as their ultimate goal.

Do I understand that someone could use some of this book's strategies to step on people? I do, but more than 30 years of experience in the workplace has taught me something crucial: Stepping on people only works short-term. Once you stab someone in the back, he or she will not forget it. In many cases, they will lay in wait for their chance to even the score—and then some. I have lived long enough to know what goes around *always* comes around, especially at work. You cannot build a life that has true meaning and be selfish at the same time.

All the rules and tools in this book can be instrumental in making you a force for positive change in your organization. But remember: You must learn and apply them. Do not simply show up for work and just do a job. You spend years of your life at work, so make it count—for yourself and for others. Be a power-broker who is able to make *good* things happen because you have built such a powerful network of supporters.

Ultimately, you have to decide what you want people to say about you, and about what you were able to do when they worked with you.

What do you want *your* legacy at work to be?

ABOUT
MARGARET MORFORD

Margaret is President for The HR Edge, Inc., an international management consulting and training company. Her clients have included Lockheed Martin, Chevron, Time Warner, U.S. Secret Service, Sara Lee Foods, Home and Garden Television, Nationwide Insurance, U.S. Department of the Treasury, NAPA Auto Parts, Homeland Security, New York Presbyterian Hospital (Cornell & Columbia Medical Centers), U.S. Marine Corps, Deloitte, Blue Cross Blue Shield, U.S. Coast Guard, Vanderbilt University, Comcast, Intercontinental Hotel Group, Small Business Administration, McKee Foods, Skanska, Fox Broadcasting, Schwarz BioSciences, Alcohol, Fire & Tobacco, Fifth Third Bank, Verizon, Northwestern Mutual Life Insurance Company, SAS (computer software), The Nashville Predators national hockey franchise, Pella Windows, Internal Revenue Service, Northrop Grumman, Miami University, Wells Fargo, The Peabody Hotel, The Hartford, TECO Energy, AmSurg, Quorum Health Resources, U.S. Naval Nuclear Submarine Group and various local and state governments. Previous to owning her own company, Margaret was Sr. Vice President, Human Resources Consulting for a national consulting firm out of Winston-Salem, North Carolina. She has a BS degree from the University of Alabama and a JD degree from the Vanderbilt University School of Law. She has worked as an attorney, specializing in employment law as well as been Vice President of Human Resources for three large companies. She serves on the Board of Directors for Aegis Sciences Corporation. She is often quoted as a business expert in newspapers and magazines across the country including *Wall Street Journal, New York Times, Chicago Tribune, USA Today* and *Entrepreneur Magazine* and appears regularly on local ABC, CBS and Fox television affiliates. She also is the author of the business book, *Management Courage: Having the Heart of a Lion.*

Margaret Morford offers seminars, workshops, presentations and speeches to organizations and business groups across North America.

For more information, please visit www.thehredge.net or contact Margaret at mmorford@thehredge.net

Breinigsville, PA USA
24 October 2010
247941BV00002B/17/P